Elizabeth Simcoe

John M. Basse

First Lady of Upper Canada

Fitzhenry & Whiteside Limited

Contents

©1974 Fitzhenry & Whiteside Limited
150 Lesmill Road
Don Mills, Ontario, M3B 2T5

Printed and bound in Canada.

ISBN 0-88902-204-6

The Atlantic Journey
Chapter 1

Outward bound from Weymouth in England to the
New World, His Majesty's man-of-war, the *Triton*,
found the going rough and stormy.

The wind roared without stopping and the waves
rolled over the ship, making any visit to the upper
decks a test of strength and determination. At times
the *Triton* rolled so far over that it appeared that she
would never right herself, but right herself she did
and, like a bulldog shaking the water from her sides,
she turned again into the wind and made some
progress, slow and uncomfortable though it was.

There were a number of officers and officials on
the *Triton*, but the most important was the new
Lieutenant-Governor of Upper Canada, Colonel John
Graves Simcoe. He was accompanied by his wife and
the two youngest of his six children. Sophia was two
years old and her brother, Francis, an infant of three
months. The four older daughters—Eliza, Charlotte,
Henrietta, and Caroline—had been left in England
under the care of two old friends, Mrs. and Miss
Hunt.

The *Triton* had left Weymouth on September 26,
1791. For forty-six days, few of them without a storm,
Mrs. Simcoe and her children had to suffer
inconvenience, poor food, and almost constant
dampness. The decks could not keep out the water,
so the beds, clothes, everything, were always wet.

But Mrs. Simcoe was a remarkable woman. She
enjoyed every new experience, welcomed every new
activity. Everything that she found of interest she put
down in her diary, and every week sent that section
of her diary to Mrs. Hunt in England to read to her
four daughters. Thanks to this diary, we have a
picture of life on the early Canadian frontier that can
be matched by few other accounts of pioneer life in
any country.

*"Captain Murray sent a boat on
board the 'Liberty' with letters
from England."*

In spite of the weather, Mrs. Simcoe tried to get on deck at least once a day, but the constant rolling of the ship soon made her sick and she retreated to the bed in her cabin.

An old sailor watched this happen a number of times and finally got up the courage to approach her.

"Excuse me, ma'am. You're having trouble getting your sea legs, I figure."

Mrs. Simcoe smiled. "I wasn't meant to be a sailor. I don't think I'll ever get over being seasick if the boat keeps rolling like this."

"You'll manage, ma'am. Take the advice of an old sailor. Don't eat anything but salt beef with plenty of mustard till you feel chipper. You'll be right as rain."

Mrs. Simcoe thanked the sailor and did as he suggested. Whatever the reason, Mrs. Simcoe was cured of her seasickness and was able to take far more interest in the voyage. It amused her to see Sophia's pleasure in watching the poultry on deck, where a little midshipman carried the small girl every day.

"So extremely cold that I could not stay on deck without a fleecy greatcoat on; a bird like a linnet and a crossbill alighted on the rigging."

As the ship approached land a variety of birds appeared, including a beautiful olive-coloured owl, no larger than a thrush. She saw porpoises and whales in the distance, as well as ships bound for Britain.

As the *Triton* slowly worked her way up the coast, everyone except Colonel Simcoe felt that they would not be able to reach Quebec before winter set in. It was already the end of October; the gales had given way to thick fog that rolled in at almost any time.

"What is the matter with the Captain?" asked Mrs. Simcoe. "He appears to be concerned about something. He never takes his eye off the sea, but I don't know what can be seen in this fog."

"That's exactly why he is so careful. Sable Island lies nearby. It is well called 'the graveyard of the Atlantic.' Thank goodness, we have a captain so aware of the danger that he must be his own watchman."

Fortunately, the ship avoided any serious delay or danger and, after sailing around Cape Breton and the island of Anticosti, the *Triton* sighted Quebec on November 10. Colonel Simcoe's optimism had been justified.

Elizabeth Chapter 2

In 1766, Elizabeth Gwillim, who was to marry John Graves Simcoe, was born in the mansion called Old Court at Whitchurch in Herefordshire, England.

The birth of a child is generally regarded as a most happy occasion. This birth could scarcely be termed that, because within twenty-four hours the mother died. Elizabeth's father, Colonel Thomas Gwillim, had died seven months before in Gibraltar.

The child was christened Elizabeth Posthuma Gwillim. The awkward middle name indicated that she had lost both her parents, but she was fortunate in having relatives eager to take care of her.

"Poor little creature," said her Aunt Margaret. "She'll never lack for anything as long as we are here to help."

Her uncle, Admiral Graves, nodded assent. "She's the child that we never had." He put his arm around his wife's shoulders. "Your sister would be happy to know that you take care of the little one."

Old Court, Herefordshire

Admiral Samuel Graves and his wife lived in a most attractive mansion, called Hembury Fort, in Devonshire. The Devon countryside is a beautiful place for a child to grow up in. Elizabeth, as she grew older, got to know the moors, with their flowers, and birds, and animals She spent many days on expeditions across the moors.

"Is it all right for her to go off on her own? She's so young and so small," worried the Admiral.

"Elizabeth can take care of herself. Don't you fret about her." Elizabeth's aunt chuckled. "She is small, but she'll not find many people she can't handle in her life."

Elizabeth soon found that she possessed remarkable skill in both painting and sketching, and on her walks on the moors got into the habit of sketching anything that took her fancy. This habit continued all her life, and to it we owe the series of drawings that so well picture life in Canada. Many of her drawings and paintings are reproduced in this book.

Her general education was not neglected. She spoke German and French fluently. Often, she spent an evening in front of a roaring fire listening to the Admiral tell his stories of adventure on the high seas, naval battles, and the interesting experiences that accompany a life aboard ship. This was a pleasant way of learning about the past.

Near the Devon town of Honiton, Admiral Graves had built a magnificent residence called Hembury Fort. Growing up in such a splendid house was most suitable for Elizabeth because she was an heiress in her own right.

In addition to her wealth, her family was one of the oldest in the country. Her ancestors included not only William the Conqueror, but also the kings who ruled Wales long before the Norman invasion. In later years, Elizabeth would often dress in Welsh costume to commemorate her ancestors.

Elizabeth's father had had a most distinguished career. He had fought as a major under General Wolfe at the Battle of the Plains of Abraham. When he died, while serving at Gibraltar, he was only thirty-five years old.

   Elizabeth had just passed her fifteenth birthday
when something happened that was to change her
entire life. Scarcely five feet tall, slightly built, she
sparkled with a good humour and vitality that
impressed everyone who met her.

   And soon to meet her was John Graves Simcoe,
godson of Admiral Graves, who had been invited to
Hembury Fort to recover after years of service and
months of captivity in the American War of
Independence.

Hembury Fort

John Chapter 3
Graves
Simcoe

For a fifteen-year-old girl, even a girl as mature as Elizabeth, the return of a wounded hero from the wars was bound to cause some concern and excitement. For a long time Elizabeth had been the centre of attention at Hembury Fort. The arrival of a tall, handsome, thirty-year-old soldier would surely change this. She did not like the idea of taking a back seat.

No one disputed Simcoe's brilliance and courage. When there were so few British successes against the Americans, Simcoe's victories were all the more notable. He had been given command of the Queen's Rangers, a famous regiment largely made up of those American settlers who had remained loyal to the British crown. Simcoe had had the vision to use their skill in woodcraft to the best advantage.

"Ay!" murmured the Admiral. "He's a brilliant officer and not afraid to do something a little different. I did hear that he had a plan to slip through the American lines, with some of his men, disguised as a group of fur traders. They were to capture General Washington himself. Probably would have done it too, but some senior officer heard of it and turned it into a big operation. Naturally, it got nowhere."

Elizabeth was unimpressed. "It didn't do him much good, did it?"

"It did, my girl. He's been given the permanent rank of lieutenant-colonel. For someone who went overseas a junior officer, a mere ensign, that is real promotion."

"Well, we were beaten, weren't we?"

A rifleman of the Queen's Rangers

"Ay, but no fault of Colonel Simcoe or the Queen's Rangers."

When the British Army was forced to surrender at Yorktown, Simcoe was one of the officers taken prisoner. However, his health was so bad that he was allowed to return to England. The doctors recommended a sea voyage as the only remedy to save his life.

Sick as he was, Simcoe never neglected the welfare and safety of the men he commanded. Since the bulk of the Queen's Rangers were native Americans, he feared that they might be regarded as traitors by their victorious compatriots. He managed to have almost all of the men smuggled aboard ships and taken to safety. His fear for his men was well founded, since twenty-five who were left behind were executed.

Later, Captain James Cook, the famous explorer.

"It's a pity he didn't join the navy," said the Admiral to Elizabeth. "His father had a brilliant career. He was captain of the sixty-gun frigate *Pembroke*. And he, with his Master, James Cook,* drew up the plans for General Wolfe's attack on Quebec. But he died young, of pneumonia, on the island of Anticosti before he heard of Wolfe's great victory."

Finally, Simcoe arrived at Hembury Fort, walking erect but pale and drawn from long illness and the effect of his wounds. Elizabeth's fears were realized. He was polite but rarely spoke to her. Most of his time was spent in front of the fire exchanging stories of battles won and lost with the Admiral.

Aunt Margaret sized up the situation. "He'll never get any colour in his cheeks, cooped up all day in a smoky room, drinking port and smoking a pipe. Elizabeth, you must take him for a walk on the moors where he'll get some fresh air."

"Yes, Aunt Margaret, if you wish." Elizabeth was not slow in extending the invitation to Simcoe. It was almost as though he too had been waiting for such an offer, which he eagerly accepted.

The walks grew longer and longer, and, as the weather improved, Elizabeth and the Colonel went riding. Both managed horses well and they ranged on day-long trips over the Devon countryside.

Wolford, near Honiton, Devon

Although the Colonel was thirty and Elizabeth only fifteen they had a great deal to talk about. Both

were well-read, both found the country a source of
interest, and both found each other's company
pleasant.

After a few months, Simcoe asked the Admiral's
permission to marry Elizabeth.

"She's so young, she's not strong at all,"grumbled
the Admiral to his wife. "Let them wait a few years."

But Aunt Margaret saw things differently. "She'll
manage very well. Indeed, she needs someone who
will take care of her. Don't forget she's wealthy and
could be married for her money. Can you think of
anyone you would rather see her marry than your
godson?"

"You're right, I'm sure. But she is still so young."

Elizabeth Posthuma Gwillim married John Graves
Simcoe in December, 1782. She was sixteen; he was
almost thirty-one.

Lieutenant- Chapter 4
Governor

Elizabeth lost no time in settling down. The first thing
to be done was to find a suitable house. But none was
just right for the kind of life that Elizabeth was
determined to lead. Both found the Devonshire
countryside to their liking, so Elizabeth bought five
thousand acres of rich farmland and built Wolford
Lodge, a forty-room mansion, on her property.

Simcoe, for his part, lost no time in plunging into
the life and activities of a country squire. As with
everything he did, he brought boundless energy to
the task. With his steward, John Scadding, he went
round the estate, always alert for what needed
improving or fixing. Just as he had done with the
Queen's Rangers, he took particular care of the people
who farmed his land.

But Elizabeth was soon aware that being a country
squire was not enough of a challenge for her
husband. The outstanding men of the day, politicians,
landowners, writers, were invited to Wolford Lodge.
Inevitably, the talk would turn to politics, and the
problem of North America was always being
discussed.

Simcoe was particularly interested in that part of
Canada where so many of his men in the Queen's
Rangers had settled.

Finally, he spoke about the subject that was
uppermost in his mind.

"I do hear, Elizabeth, that the province of Quebec
is to be divided into two parts, with the new part to
be run according to British law and the British form of
government. I also hear that there is a search right
now for a lieutenant-governor for the province."

"And you'd like to be that governor?" asked
Elizabeth.

"It would mean hardship for you and separation from our family if I was offered the position, but I know the country, I know the people. I'm sure I could do what must be done."

"I know you could," Elizabeth replied. "I'll do everything I can to help you."

What abilities does John Graves Simcoe show that make him a wise choice for the first Lieutenant-Governor of Upper Canada?

No doubt the principal reason for choosing Simcoe was his magnificent record in the American War. But perhaps Elizabeth's enthusiasm also had something to do with it. In 1791, Simcoe was appointed the first Lieutenant-Governor of Upper Canada.

Winter in Chapter 5
Canada

Finally, the long journey was over. Elizabeth Simcoe hardly knew what to expect in the New World. Her usually optimistic nature, however, could scarcely stand the disappointment of her first view of Canada.

The *Triton* put into Quebec City on November 11, 1791. A mixture of rain and snow was falling, the sky was overcast, and from the ship the town looked like a dismal collection of huts.

"I'm not going ashore to that miserable little place," she complained to her husband.

"Well, my dear, if you don't, you'll have a long spell aboard ship. We can't continue to Upper Canada until next spring."

Elizabeth's attitude soon changed. Before the day was out she was on shore eagerly noting the differences in the life around her. For the first time in her life she rode in a sleigh. The horses whisked the carriole over the snow and, bundled in furs, she was quickly carried to her house. But late one evening, returning from a supper party, she found it so cold that she wore a fencing mask lined with fur. On another occasion, Elizabeth called the drive "very jolty."

Canadian Carrole safe & pleasant

"*From hence I went in an open carriole (which is a sort of phaeton body on a sledge or runners, shod with iron instead of wheels).*"

Even the first meal was worth noting: partridge tastier than she had ever had before and apples that had the flavour of strawberries.

Indoors, the cold was no problem. Indeed, as many visitors to Canada have noted down to our day, the houses were kept uncomfortably warm and Elizabeth was constantly opening windows to cool off the room.

Elizabeth and her husband went on long walks. A favourite one was to Cape Diamond, a distance of about three miles. By wrapping herself in furs, and wearing coarse stockings over her shoes to prevent slipping, she found that winter was to be enjoyed, not feared.

"Do you realize," she asked her husband, "it was twenty-three degrees below zero yesterday? And no matter how cold it gets, we never seem to be sick."

There was a constant round of parties and dinners and dances, so many, in fact, that Elizabeth found that a number had to be refused. Prince Edward,* the young son of King George III, was at Quebec, and with the senior officers of the army and the many titled administrators, society was gay and colourful. Two days after Christmas, Elizabeth wrote: "I was at a very pleasant ball at the Chateau, and danced with Prince Edward."

Afterwards Duke of Kent, father of Queen Victoria.

Elizabeth's letters and diary were full of descriptions of the interesting and novel things in the town, to entertain her daughters in England. Dogs pulling sleds laden with provisions intrigued her. She wrote of the strange food, such as moose lip and coxcomb pie.

Write a brief account of life in Quebec during the winter.

She visited the Montmorency Falls and admired the summer house that had been built projecting over the water.

But her enthusiasm was matched by Simcoe's impatience. "When can we get started on our way? I'm tired of Quebec and its parties. There's so much to be done and here I am doing nothing."

Slowly the weather improved, and finally enough members of the newly appointed council arrived in Quebec to make plans for the governing of the new province.

Upper Canada had come into being at December 26, 1791.

Finally, on June 5, the Simcoes left Quebec and continued on their voyage in three large bateaux.

Chapter 6 Upper Canada

Elizabeth was not sorry to leave Quebec. True, she had made many good friends. It seemed that the whole winter had been one whirl of dances, dinners and supper parties. But, like her husband, she was eager to get to the new province and see the new frontier.

"It will be a pleasant journey for you and the children," said the Governor. "I'm told that riding in one of the bateau can be most enjoyable."

And most of the time it was a pleasant way to travel. The men paddling the bateau would break into song and keep time to the strokes of the paddles. They were the same songs sung by the voyageurs who crossed half a continent to trade for furs with the Indians.

Another blessing was the absence of mosquitoes on the river. However, whenever the boat approached shore a horde of vicious mosquitoes would descend on the travellers. The only relief at night was to sit around the fire but, as the weather got hotter and hotter, this became a real hardship.

In Montreal, the temperature rose to ninety-six degrees. A sentinel, seeing the futile attempts of Elizabeth to gain some relief, turned to her and said, "There's but a sheet of brown paper between this place and hell." Elizabeth was bound to agree.

Fortunately, the party were invited to stay at Government House. This building, erected in 1705, is still standing. Its thick stone walls and high ceilings gave a measure of coolness not found elsewhere. Now called the Chateau de Ramezay, it may well be the oldest building in Canada.

Chateau de Ramezay, Montreal

Not all the stopping places were as pleasant as this. Some of the inns were dirty and uncomfortable, and Elizabeth would unroll a blanket and try to sleep

on the floor. She spent one night sleeping on a table.
She was glad to return to the comfort of the bateau.
As she progressed up the river, rapids became more
and more frequent. When this happened, they were
forced to take to carriages and suffer the misery of
being bounced over impossible roads or, when
available, ride on one of the sure-footed horses that
took them over the worst country.

Some of the bridges were simply tree trunks
spanning the streams. A horse could easily break a leg
on such a bridge, but with amazing skill they always
seemed to find the log that would support them.

Finally, some of the inns were so dirty and
disreputable that Elizabeth refused to sleep in them.
For the first time the tent was pitched and
immediately it was found to be most comfortable.
Little did Elizabeth realize that for the next two years
the tent was to be her permanent residence.

The travellers soon reached Kingston. This was a
settlement of about fifty wooden houses, and by far
the biggest town in Upper Canada.

*"We rose very early in the
morning in order to take a view
of the mill at Gananoque."*

"Will you make this the capital of the new province?" Elizabeth asked the Governor.

"The people here would like it, but there are too many reasons against it. The new capital must be central; it must be capable of being defended, which this is not; and the harbour here is impossible. It opens up to the westerly winds. An enemy could bottle us up here at will. No, my dear, I am afraid Kingston is not suitable."

But the Governor enjoyed being at Kingston. He went sailing, inspected fortifications, and his beloved Queen's Rangers were stationed just outside the town. In addition, the members of the council had gathered there and so Simcoe was able to take the oath of office.

Trace the Simcoes' trip from Quebec to the Niagara River.

"We shall travel in greater comfort for the last part of the voyage." He pointed to one of the two schooners riding in the bay. "That is the *Onondaga*, commanded by Commodore Beaton. He will take us to Niagara."

The last part of the trip took only two days and was quite uneventful. On the second day, clear and cold in spite of the fact that it was mid-July, Elizabeth could see the spray of Niagara Falls in the distance.

"The 'Onondaga' was left under the care of a young lieutenant and ran aground. It is feared she cannot be got off until the Spring, and then perhaps not without injury."

Life at Chapter 7
Niagara

"The cloud you see in the distance, ma'am, really is the mist rising from the falls at Niagara," said Commodore Beaton.

Everyone crowded to the rail to see what was to be their home for some years. Slowly the *Onondaga* approached the Niagara River and as it entered the mouth of the river everyone was struck by the beauty of the surrounding cliffs.

Elizabeth could scarcely wait to get ashore. "It's beautiful. I've never seen a more majestic sight in my whole life. I've never seen taller or more striking trees. This will be a wonderful place to live," and she turned to her husband. "It will also be a wonderful place for the capital of your new province."

Colonel Simcoe did not reply. He was gazing intently at the shoreline. Finally he turned to the Commodore, "I understood that there were some excellent buildings in this area. All I can see are four very poor buildings. Is this all?"

"Ay, Colonel. They are called Navy Hall but are scarcely fit for a lady or gentleman to sleep in. Perhaps we could rig up a marquee from sailcloth until something more suitable is built. The weather will stay warm for a good time yet."

"Do that, Commodore. In any case, we are well supplied with some sound tents and we can make do with them till something fitting is built."

Colonel Simcoe was proud of his tents. They had originally belonged to Captain Cook, his father's close friend, who had used them on his voyage to the South Seas. They were to be of greater service to Elizabeth and her family.

Everyone was anxious to visit the great falls that they had heard so much about and so within three days of landing at the mouth of the Niagara River

"At nine this morning we anchored at Navy Hall, opposite the garrison of Niagara. Navy Hall is a house built by the naval commanders of this lake."

they set out. Because the current was so fast and because there were dangerous rapids near the falls, it was necessary to go by caleche, a two-wheeled, horse-drawn carriage.

On the way they stopped at the home of Robert Hamilton, a prominent citizen of Niagara. Elizabeth was most impressed by the building. "That surely must be the finest home in all of Upper Canada. It's built of solid stone, and look at the balcony! It goes the whole length of the house and must give a wonderful view of the river."

The Hamiltons joined the party to the falls. Even though they expected a magnificent view, the newcomers had not anticipated anything so impressive. The falls stretched in a huge semicircle over which the waters tumbled for almost two hundred feet before striking the rocks below.

"Mr. Hamilton has a very good stone house, the back rooms overlooking on the river. A gallery, the length of the house, is a delightful covered walk."

"You can get a much more striking view from Table Rock, if you would care to climb down," suggested Mr. Hamilton.

Elizabeth looked over the edge of the river, and started back, as the sight made her quite giddy. However, little could stop Elizabeth and, holding firmly to Mr. Hamilton, she made her way down to the rock. From there, the great mass of water was an even more striking sight than from above. One had to glance up to see the river curl over the edge of the falls and start its plunge downwards. It was difficult to be heard over the roar of the water, and the mist from the falls hung about them; but in spite of their position someone managed to boil water for tea, and the party sat on Table Rock sipping the refreshing drink.

Elizabeth returned to the falls whenever the opportunity presented itself. She was always welcome at the Hamiltons' and appreciated the chance to sleep in a fine house once in a while.

Life had its problems on the frontier and Elizabeth Simcoe had her particular worries; but she kept a sense of humour that made the inconveniences appear small.

One day she returned to the tent to find her best map of Canada and the United States, which she had spent so long drawing, ripped to shreds by her dog, Trojan. Colonel Simcoe, a loving husband but an indifferent poet, "made some very pretty verses on the occasion."

Shortly afterwards she received a complete set of fine china from England. Such luxuries were rare on the frontier. Carefully it was unpacked, carefully it was put out in a small bower beside the tent, but the wood caught fire and, in the effort to save the tent, almost all the chinaware was destroyed.

Log huts or barracks at Queenston

"We are in daily expectation of the Prince. The canvas houses are not yet arrived or Navy Hall finished."

Even though they were hundreds of miles from any town of size, visitors constantly found their way to the Niagara River. Prince Edward made the long journey, and there was great excitement as they prepared for a succession of entertainments. However, misfortune struck as the Prince was landing. Colonel Simcoe, dressed in formal uniform, stood ready to welcome the visitor. Unfortunately, he was standing too near the cannon that were fired in honour of the Prince's arrival. The cannon fire deafened the Governor, and so severe was the pain in his head that he could scarcely stand. He had to stay in bed for two weeks, and by that time the Prince had gone.

Another visitor was the Indian Chief, Thayendanegea, more commonly known as Joseph Brant. He made a striking figure in a handsome silk blanket trimmed with gold carelessly thrown over his uniform. He had once been to England and spent some time with the King.

"I don't trust him," Elizabeth confided to her husband. "He has a cunning look." But in this case Mrs. Simcoe's judgment was wrong. Brant was a loyal supporter of the British.

"Captain Brant (Thayendanegea), Chief of the Six Nations dined here."

"On the American side the river passing over a straight ledge of rock has not the beauty of the circular form or its green colour, the whole centre of the circular falls being of the brightest green, and below it frequently seen a rainbow."

Chapter 8 The First Year at Niagara

Elizabeth soon grew accustomed to life on the frontier. Fortunately, the first winter was quite mild. The tent served very well as a house. Colonel Simcoe had had it divided by a canvas wall and when Elizabeth wanted privacy she had only to enter the inner room.

With a wooden roof to keep off the snow, the "canvas house" was quite warm. Here Elizabeth could write her journal and letters, to send home to England. Here too she did her drawing and reading, so that her days were full.

Elizabeth was a talented woman. She enjoyed books, and sat up all one night reading Spanish poetry and history. But drawing remained her major interest. Although she says that she never painted a

"In camp near Queenston"

place that she did not wish to remember, she was always sketching. She got up very early one summer morning to "take a view" of some exceptionally pretty scenery and felt well rewarded for the effort. She saw everything with an artist's eye. On one journey she passed a group of Indians sitting round a fire near a river, "which in this dark night afforded a good subject for a picture." The dark air, filled with fireflies, appeared "beautiful like falling stars." She also kept her youthful love of flowers, which she mentions again and again, and these she paints with words: "I gathered a very sweet and pretty white flower, the petals of the texture of orange flowers, five petals, ten chives, tipped with orange colour, the style pink, the leaves a light green." Nothing escaped her notice.

Almost every week there was a ball: "There were fourteen couples, a great display of gauze, feathers and velvet, the room lighted by wax candles, and there was a supper, as well as tea." When the evenings dragged, there was always a group to play whist.

January 16, 1793 a sixth daughter was born. She was called Katherine and seemed a remarkably healthy child.

Colonel Simcoe, with a small party of soldiers, set out in January to walk to Detroit. Once again the weather was pleasant and the long walk proved to be most enjoyable. The Indians in the party would go ahead and prepare the fire and rough huts for sleeping. In exactly five weeks the Governor returned. He was most enthusiastic about La Tranche River.

"I've changed its name to the river Thames and, just like the Thames in England, this river will have the capital city on its banks. Oh, I know that there is nothing there yet but some Indian tents, but the situation is perfect. It's right in the centre of Upper Canada. It's well away from the United States, and the soil will make it the richest farmland in the whole country."

"When do you propose setting up your capital?" asked Elizabeth.

"Not for some time. Indeed, not for many years. But we must move from here. With only a river a few

Governor Simcoe was anxious to have the capital of the new province at present-day London, Ontario. Would it have been a good or poor choice?

hundred yards wide separating us from a foreign country, we are in a most dangerous position, a most insecure position."

Spring came quickly that year and with it most unseasonably hot weather. The Simcoe's son, Francis, became sick. Fortunately, the Hamiltons invited Elizabeth and her children to stay with them. The stone house on the edge of the escarpment was much cooler and Francis quickly recovered.

Elizabeth's dog, Trojan, was not so lucky. It began acting strangely, perhaps because of the heat, but a nervous soldier, afraid of rabies, shot it. Even the Governor's dog had its share of bad luck. It made the foolish mistake of trying to bite a porcupine.

Finally, the Governor, after a hurried trip to Toronto, came to a decision. "For the time being we shall move our capital there."

"Walked along the river half a mile to a beautiful spot among the rocks. The rapid clear water has a fine effect."

Toronto Chapter 9

It was a warm July morning when the ship *Mississaga* carefully entered Toronto Harbour. Everyone was impressed by the beauty of the scene, but no one more than Mrs. Simcoe.

"I have never seen a more magnificent stand of oak than that along the shore. And see how crystal-clear the water is."

By the time Colonel Simcoe arrived a few days later, Elizabeth had already explored much of the nearby countryside. Sometimes on horseback, sometimes by canoe, and sometimes on foot, they covered a great area.

"As no person on board had ever been in Toronto, Mr. Bouchette was afraid to enter the harbour until daylight."

A spit of low-lying land provided a perfect natural protection for the harbour. On one of their walks along the sand, the Governor pointed to the end of the spit, "Put some guns there and no navy on earth could get by them. That's as strong as Gibraltar itself. Indeed we could call it Gibraltar Point and not be greatly amiss."

To the east, the most striking feature was the white cliffs towering over the lake. It was Elizabeth this time who was reminded of a similar sight in England. "John, have you ever seen anything more like the white chalk cliffs at Scarborough?"

"Not chalk, but sand; but you are right. They are very much like them. Would that not make a suitable place for a summer house?"

Two small, navigable rivers, the Humber and the Don, flowed into the lake nearby. Both were attractive but the Don was the most interesting. High hills rose up on either side. In places, huge trees had fallen, spanning the river so that they formed natural bridges under which the canoes could pass.

The first time that Elizabeth saw the hills she knew that this was the place for their summer home. "On top of one of those hills. That's the spot."

"The spot for what?" asked her husband.

"Why, for our summer home. Any one of those

"There were a party of Ojibway Indians here. One of them named 'Great Sail' took Francis in his arms, and was much pleased to find the child was not afraid."

hills would be perfect. The view will be magnificent and there should always be a breeze for my little Francis, who does suffer so much from the heat."

Work soon started on the house. There was no delay in naming the place. "We'll call it Castle Frank, after Francis. He'll like it here."

Indeed, Francis did thrive in Toronto. There were so many things to please an active child and, now that he could walk, so many things to explore.

A band of Ojibway visited them and, with their air of marked superiority, made an immediate impression. They wore handsome silver brooches, colourful armbands and scarlet leggings. Chief Canise, or "Great Sail," offered the Governor a magnificent blanket made of beaver skins.

Francis watched the ceremony of the exchange of gifts till he could restrain himself no longer and ran to Canise. The Indian lifted him high in the air and, as the guns roared out in salute, both burst into gales of laughter.

Canise returned the lad to Elizabeth. "A fine boy. A brave warrior." Canise's words were to prove prophetic because Francis was to fall in the attack on Badajoz in Spain during the Peninsular War.

Elizabeth too was impressed by the Indians. "When they speak," she said, "they resemble what I imagine the Greek and Roman orators must have been."

An excellent location for Castle Frank had been chosen. It was on the highest point in the area and it was possible to look down on the top of some of the huge butternut trees in the valley of the Don and even see the nests that the eagles had built.

The family still used the tent, although sometimes they spent the night at Castle Frank with a roaring fire in both huge fireplaces.

Colonel Simcoe busied himself in the work that he loved. Two highways were carved out of the wilderness. Dundas Street went through to London, and Yonge Street went up to Lake Simcoe, named after his father.

Toronto was renamed York, to honour the Duke of York, the King's second son.

The second winter passed quickly. Elizabeth and
the Governor by now had adopted many of the local
customs—ice skating, ice fishing and, in the spring,
making maple sugar.

With spring, the family returned to Niagara.

*"The Governor determined to
take a lot of 200 acres upon the
River Don for Francis, and to
build a house upon it."*

First official plan of York
(Toronto), 1793

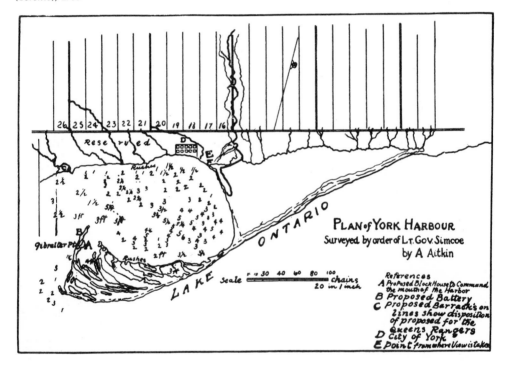

Friends Chapter 10
of the
Simcoes

The contrast between the handsome estate in Devon that the Simcoes had left and the frontier that they had come to was indeed immense. However, as Governor of the new province of Upper Canada, Simcoe was able to provide many benefits for his wife and children. Certainly, Elizabeth led a life far different from that of the average frontier woman.

Sometimes it seemed that there was a never ending round of whist, and when that was finished there were balls and dinners to attend. Indeed, so numerous were the balls, that Elizabeth found that she could not attend them all. The American Commissioners who had come to Canada about Indian affairs remarked on the beauty and charm of the ladies—wives of officers stationed at the Niagara Garrison—who surrounded the Governor's wife.

In this chapter, and in other parts of the book, friends of the Simcoes are introduced. Briefly tell why you find some of them interesting.

The Simcoes, it is true, spent their first two winters in their famous "canvas house." Perhaps this was through choice, because some of the truly fine houses along the Niagara River were open to them, and we have seen that when Francis was suffering from the heat he spent some weeks in the Hamilton home.

Another house, even larger, was that of David William Smith, Surveyor-General of Upper Canada, and here too the Governor and his family were welcome.

"I went to see Mr. Smith's house he has built on this side of the river. It is a very good one."

The Simcoes had a large staff of servants, and when Elizabeth cooked it was because she enjoyed cooking, or wanted a special dish, such as her famous chowder of salmon, pork and biscuit.

Among their friends were some brilliant men. One

was William Osgoode, who had been appointed Chief Justice of Upper Canada and was responsible for the Constitution of the new province. The first Provincial Secretary was William Jarvis. One of Toronto's main streets is named after him.

Accompanying Governor Simcoe as his private and confidential secretary was Lieutenant Thomas Talbot. He was a young man of tremendous energy and initiative. He immediately fell in love with the country and was eager to try any new experience that it offered. He soon became the best skater of the entire company. His skill at ice fishing almost matched that of the Indians. He learned to paddle a canoe so skilfully that it slid noiselessly and almost without effort through the water. He was recalled to England in 1794 to serve with his regiment in the war against France, but returned to Canada seven years later and was given title to five thousand acres of land near Lake Erie. Known as the Talbot Settlement, it was most successful and had a population of forty thousand.

Mr. Talbot's House

"He brought with him Mr. Talbot, a relation of Lady Buckingham at whose request Colonel Simcoe takes Mr. Talbot into his family."

John Scadding, who had been manager of the Simcoe estate at Wolford, followed the Simcoes out to Canada in much the same role. He too returned later to Canada and took possession of a tract of land in what is now downtown Toronto. The first cottage that he built burnt down but he replaced it with a sturdy log cabin in 1794. The cabin still stands today in the grounds of the Canadian National Exhibition and is by far the oldest building in Toronto.

John Scadding's son, Henry, came to Canada when he was only eleven. He became Principal of Upper Canada College and later Rector of Holy Trinity. The house he built there still stands. Where once the Reverend Henry Scadding wrote his scholarly articles, children now throng at the first children's centre for the arts in Toronto.

The Indians too were friendly and helpful. Perhaps it was because the Simcoes treated them with respect and dignity. Governor Simcoe was given the Indian name, Deyonguhokrawen, which means "One Whose Door Is Always Open."

Henry Scadding

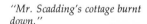

"Mr. Scadding's cottage burnt down."

Chapter 11 **Return to Niagara**

The Simcoe family were about to return to Niagara when tragedy struck. Their infant daughter, Katherine, their only child to be born in Canada, died suddenly. Just fifteen months old, she gave every indication of being the healthiest child imaginable. Not only was she attractive, but even at that early age showed that she possessed a most cheerful temperament. The loss was a severe blow to Elizabeth.

Francis' health, which was frequently poor, now became a matter of grave concern to his mother. A friend advised Elizabeth to give him crowsfoot boiled with milk to cure a stomach upset.

Parliament still had its meetings in Niagara since it was the only place with buildings sufficiently large to hold the members. The first parliament had met in 1792 and this was to be the third one. Governor

The First Parliament of Upper Canada

Simcoe had insisted on having all the pageantry and colour that was associated with the event back in England. A guard of honour, made up of Simcoe's own Queen's Rangers, handsome in their scarlet tunics, was drawn up outside Navy Hall. The boats in the river fired a royal salute and the band struck up "God Save the King."

While parliament sat only a few weeks each summer, much had been accomplished. Most important was the adoption of the British systems of justice and civil matters that the settlers were accustomed to.

In 1793, a Bill was passed that led to the speedy freeing of the slaves. This parliament was one of the first in the entire world to pass such humane legislation.

Making their way slowly along the shore of the lake, the Simcoes took four days to get from York to Niagara. Scarcely had they reached Niagara than Elizabeth exclaimed, "We've only been here two hours and I wish we were back at York. It was never so hot and humid there. There was always some breeze to cool us."

That summer was almost unbearable. Even such a firm believer in ceremony as Governor Simcoe was forced to make some concession to the heat. He had the members of the Legislature conduct their business outside under a huge oak tree. The tree, which stood until a few years ago, was called Parliament Oak, and though the tree has gone, a school on the same site is named Parliament Oak in its memory.

Why was Governor Simcoe so intent on having the meetings of the Legislature accompanied with all the pomp and ceremony possible? What was achieved at these early parliaments?

After the opening of parliament in 1793, Lieutenant Talbot organized one of the most successful balls in the new province's history. Dancing continued till midnight, followed by a magnificent dinner. Mrs. Simcoe did not dance but watched with interest the twenty-two couples who did. The party did not break up till three in the morning.

In spite of the fact that she lived on the very edge of the wilderness, Elizabeth Simcoe had little time to be bored. Every year that the Simcoes were in Niagara a steady stream of visitors passed through and

The Duke de La Rochefoucauld

"Their appearance is perfectly democratic and dirty. I dislike them all."

Why, in the year 1795, did Mrs. Simcoe connect dirt with democracy?

"Mr. Mackenzie who has made his way from the Grand Portage to the Pacific Ocean, is just returned from thence."

provided both a source of interest and news of the outside world.

One such visitor was the French Duke de la Rochefoucauld. A political exile from his native country, he was on a visit to the United States, and of course no such visit would be complete without seeing the famous falls at Niagara.

Like so many other travellers, the Duke wrote a book about his experiences and in it described Elizabeth:

Mrs. Simcoe is a lady of thirty-six years of age. She is bashful and speaks little; but she is a woman of sense, handsome and amiable, and fulfils all the duties of a mother and wife with the most scrupulous exactness. The performance of the latter she carries so far as to act the part of a private secretary to her husband. Her talent for drawing, the practice of which she confines to maps and plans, enables her to be extremely useful to the Governor.

Now, we might consider this a compliment to Elizabeth, but in those days to suggest a gentlewoman did any kind of work was an insult. For her part, Elizabeth said bluntly that she disliked the Duke and his gentlemen and described their appearance as "perfectly democratic and dirty."

Another and much more welcome visitor was the great explorer, Alexander Mackenzie. Some years before he had traced the Mackenzie River to its mouth and now was returning from his expedition to the Pacific Coast.

He had many stories to tell of the Coast Indians: "They never taste meat in their entire lives. Indeed they fear that if any meat is thrown in the water all the fish will leave. One of my men chanced to toss a bone in the ocean, and in a second an Indian had jumped in and cast it out.

"Please accept, ma'am," continued Mackenzie, "this fur of the sea otter. It is a great rarity and most highly prized by the Indians."

The first Protestant Bishop of Quebec, Bishop Mountain, also paid the Simcoes a visit. This man laboured in the New World for thirty-two years to establish the Anglican Church. When he arrived there were only six clergymen to help him. By the time he died he had established his church throughout Upper and Lower Canada.

One day, a band of about fifty Seneca Indians

landed from their canoes and encamped outside the
paling. Elizabeth was most impressed by the quiet
way they walked and their ease of movement. "Never
do they make a motion that does not effect the
purpose that they intend."

Francis, of course, was delighted to see any
Indians. All the time that was allowed, he spent with
the band, singing their songs and trying to follow
them in their dances.

Just about this time, Francis had his third birthday.
One of the soldiers prepared a twenty-one-gun salute
for him. The guns were less than two inches long but
they gave a most satisfactory bang and pleased
Francis a great deal.

Governor Simcoe suffered another of the annoying
accidents that seemed to plague him. As he was
walking near the Indian camp, a soldier fired at an
Indian dog which was making off with a piece of
pork. One of the shots wounded the dog, another
piece hit an Indian, and yet a third hit the Governor
in the finger. Simcoe never regained the use of that
finger. Only with a great effort did the Governor
restrain his temper. However, he reprimanded the
soldier for his carelessness and, to placate the Indian,
had the soldier give him his gun immediately.

Bishop Mountain

Chapter 12 **War Clouds**

Hardly had the Simcoes returned to Niagara before a new source of worry arose. Every traveller brought rumours of American preparations for war against Canada. The Americans felt that they had more than one grievance against the British, and Canada was, of course, the place where such grievances would be avenged.

Dundas Street, the road that Simcoe had cut through the forest from York to the River Thames, was in constant use. It was but another example of Simcoe's foresight in preparing Canada for any eventuality. The troops that could be spared were moved from York to Detroit, and although the British were terribly weak in artillery, cannon from both York and Niagara were sent to the threatened fort.

The principal cause of the Americans' anger was the forts still held by the British on the frontier, and the fort that offended them the most was the one at Detroit. Simcoe had not wanted the fort built but he was ordered to build it by Lord Dorchester, Governor of Lower Canada and Governor-in-Chief of British North America.

Simcoe felt that building such a fort, in such a place, would be regarded by the Americans as an aggressive act, since it would become a threat to their traders and a haven for enemy Indians.

He was quite right. The Americans set out to destroy the fort. Any such attack would bring war to the entire frontier. The American General, "Mad Anthony" Wayne, brought his troops up ready to attack. However, the sight of so many cannon, so many British regulars, and so many enemy Indians made him stop and consider. After due consideration he decided to withdraw.

War had been avoided by the narrowest possible

General "Mad Anthony" Wayne

margin, but everyone knew that the next time such an incident occured, the outcome could easily be different. The Niagara frontier was no place for the Governor's wife and children at such a time, so arrangements were speedily made to move the family to Quebec City. The Governor in the meantime would visit the trouble spot at Detroit.

In mid-September Elizabeth with her two children set sail on board the *Mississaga*.

"It would be better to stay on shore till the boat is ready to sail," suggested the Captain.

"Thank you," replied Elizabeth, "but I prefer to board the ship now. I have seen too many ships miss a fair wind because they had to wait for a late passenger."

Elizabeth's decision proved wise. They were scarcely settled on board ship before a favourable wind came up and the *Mississaga* headed for Kingston.

As the ship gained headway Elizabeth looked back at the small town of Niagara and the mighty river behind it. "It's a beautiful place. Pray God, we shall soon return with no danger of war either to spoil it or endanger the lives of our soldiers."

"A very rough night. At eight this morning we anchored in Kingston Harbour."

Violent storms came up but, in spite of the
buffeting that the *Mississaga* took, she reached
Kingston in less than two days.

After Kingston, the journey was continued by
bateaux. Still the heavy rains continued, and as they
passed the Long Sault, storms rocked the small boats.
For a time it appeared they must either capsize or be
carried across the river to the American shore. Sophia
and Francis were both crying with fright, and even
Elizabeth was worried. However, the men at the oars
finally overcame the force of the winds and the boat
was able to land on the Canadian shore.

Captain David Cowan, one of the prosperous
settlers in the area, put them up in his fine house.
"Fortunate that you weren't driven onto the American
shore, ma'am. Nasty rebels they are, over there. Can't
tell what would happen."

Elizabeth and her family reached Quebec City only
eighteen days after leaving Niagara; much faster than
the trip four years before to Niagara.

But even in those four years, Elizabeth noticed
many changes. Both Kingston and Montreal had
grown much larger. Wooden shacks in many places
had given way to handsome stone houses. More land
was cleared and cultivated and crops were much more
abundant.

The accommodation too was generally much
better. Both at Three Rivers and Cap Santé, Elizabeth
stayed at the same place she had stopped at on the
way down. Both times she was moved by the
welcome offered her.

Finally, on October 1, she reached Quebec. A
house had been made available for her, and as she
prepared to spend the winter there news came of a
peace treaty between the United States of America
and Great Britain.

"I would dearly love to return to Niagara and be
with the Governor, but I dare not take my children on
such a trip in wintertime."

Quebec

Chapter 13

Elizabeth was worried about her husband but she
knew that such separations were inevitable. As
though to help her forget the separation, she was
given an endless round of invitations to dinners and
dances. She also went out to breakfast and tea, and
one morning had "22 visitors."

She rented a house on Palace Street but was there
so infrequently that she never describes it in her
diary. She also bought a covered carriole. The trim
sleighs had first caught her attention when she had
just landed in Canada, and now she had one of her
own to whisk her from one fine house to another.

Lord and Lady Dorchester both took a strong
liking to Elizabeth, and she was a constant visitor to
the Chateau, the Governor's residence. Elizabeth
loved the big parties that were held there, with as
many as sixty guests at one time. Perhaps it was
because Lady Dorchester wished that her guests were
not so formal that she appreciated the gay and
fun-loving Elizabeth.

She was an even more frequent visitor at her
friends, the Caldwells. (Colonel Caldwell had been a
friend of Elizabeth's father.) They lived at Belmont, a
house four miles from Quebec. Now that she had her
carriole, two days rarely passed without her visiting
them. In the short space of fifteen days she was a
guest at the Chateau four times, visited Belmont five
times, played whist three times, and "drank tea"
twice.

*"Lady Dorchester was so
obliging to insist on sending me
one of her carrioles."*

But pleasant as these parties were, Elizabeth
anxiously waited for news from her husband, and at
length the welcome message came. The danger of war
had passed and Elizabeth was to meet the Colonel at
Johnstown, just over the Quebec border.

Lord Dorchester showed Elizabeth a type of sleigh
well suited to such a trip as this in the midst of
winter. The sleigh was so designed that the traveller

could sleep in it at night if there was no suitable accommodation available. Hence its name— *dormeuse*. Elizabeth describes it as similar to "an open carriole, with a head made of sealskin, and lined with baize; a large bear or buffalo skin fixes in front, which perfectly secures you from wind or weather, and may be unhooked if the weather is fine or mild; a low seat and feather bed keep one's feet warm."

Elizabeth liked it so much that she ordered one to be made for her, and on February 6 set off to meet Governor Simcoe.

Lord Dorchester sent word ahead that there were to be horses ready for her at every post house on the road. Because of this, the three sleighs in the party made good time, but Elizabeth was worried about the thickness of the ice whenever it was necessary to travel over water. A sudden thaw could make the ice rotten in a matter of a few hours, and there were plenty of stories to frighten her. Just three days before her arrival, near Gananoque, a settler had lost two horses by being too far from shore. He had managed to save the carriole by cutting the traces but had not been nimble enough to throw a rope around the horses' heads and pull them to safety.

A more tragic story concerned a traveller crossing Lake Champlain. He noticed a large hole in the ice and an infant, alive, lying beside it. It was supposed that a sleigh, heavily laden with a large family, had broken through the ice. The mother had probably thrown the child to safety as the sleigh went down.

Life Chapter 14
on the
Frontier

The time for the departure of Governor Simcoe and his family from Canada was fast approaching. Life was becoming much more pleasant for all. Not only was the entire family getting accustomed to life on the frontier, but tremendous strides had been made in improving living conditions, in building houses, making roads, and increasing crops in the fields.

Elizabeth still found a great deal to appeal to her curiosity. She was ready to believe almost any story that she heard about this wonderful land.

Birds and animals were a source of amazement. She had seen the flocks of carrier pigeons fly overhead in such vast numbers that they cut out the sun's rays. She had also seen the ease with which they were killed. A stick thrown into the flock would bring down a number of dead pigeons. She had heard that some men tied a bullet to a long string. Whirling this makeshift weapon overhead the hunters brought down the pigeons by the thousands. It is sad to think that this beautiful bird that once darkened our skies is now extinct.

Deer were also plentiful in the Niagara district. The Indians would encircle a huge area with logs. The deer would regard it as a fence and, fearing to step over the logs, were slaughtered. Elizabeth heard of five hundred being killed in this manner.

Elizabeth was also always willing to try the foods of the country. She tasted her first wild turkey and found it excellent. She also enjoyed the melons that grew so abundantly. She tried Indian corn both boiled and roasted, as we do today. The May apples were considered a luxury, as were the blueberries that she calls "hurtleberries."

We have seen that the whole Simcoe family were sick at one time or another. It was certainly not because they lacked remedies. Elizabeth found catmint in tea helped to settle the stomach, and "sweet marjorie" tea good for a headache. She discovered that boiling water poured over the sumac flower gave a drink very much like lemon juice.

Everyone looked forward to the spring run of

The Gorge at Forty Mile Creek, near Grimsby

"There are a hundred people settled at the Forty, and there have been but seven graves in five years."

maple syrup. Like everything else that is in demand,
the price rose steadily and Mrs. Simcoe felt she was
being overcharged when she paid three dollars for
thirty pounds.

Francis was a source of constant pride and
amusement. He continued to make friends with every
Indian whom he saw, and invariably they treated him
kindly and respectfully. While on a day's outing at
Fort Erie, they came across a small party of Indians
washing their clothes on flat rocks near the shore.
Francis solemnly watched them as he sat on an
adjacent rock and when the Indians had finished,
soaking wet though he was, he asked his mother for a
loaf of bread to give to his new friends.

Francis was popular with almost everybody. The
servants built him a small cart and trained a goat to
pull it. It became one of Francis' duties to haul the
firewood to the house. Elizabeth admired the goat and
its fine harness. She thought it was the most
handsome goat that she had ever seen. She thought
Francis handsome, too.

The last winter that the Simcoes spent in Canada
was at York. They were bitterly disappointed that
Castle Frank was not completed. Indeed, it seemed
that the workmen hired to build the house were a
most irresponsible lot.

On one occasion Elizabeth says that one of the
men built himself a cottage while he should have been
working on Castle Frank. Another workman proudly
displayed the canoe he had built for himself while
neglecting his proper job.

Elizabeth showed her interest in the building by
making at least half a dozen drawings of it. The large
pine trees made pillars for the porticoes and from the
distance gave the impression that a Greek temple had
been transported into the Canadian wilds. Even
though the building was not complete, the Simcoes
spent a great deal of time there, and as soon as the
weather permitted, their visits were still more
frequent.

The Governor now frequently found that he could
take a day away from his duties and spend it with his
family. They built an Indian ladder so that they could
see the Niagara Falls better. An Indian ladder was

made from a tall cedar tree, with the branches cut off about a foot from the trunk. With such a ladder they were able to descend into the gorge to get a different view of the falls.

Once when the family was on its way to Fort Erie, they stopped at a fine house that they took to be an inn. So pleasant was it that they stayed there for almost six hours, ordered dinner and generally enjoyed themselves. Their surprise may be imagined when they found out that what they thought was an inn was in reality a farmhouse owned by a very hospitable farmer.

"Dined at Mrs. Tice's and obtained her consent to staying a fortnight in her house."

Farewells Chapter 15

The Simcoes spent the winter of 1795/6 in York. Both knew that their stay in Canada was coming to an end, but both pursued their interests with as much vigour as they had displayed on their arrival.

The Governor and his wife returned to Niagara for the sitting of the Legislature in 1795 and 1796. At the latter meeting it became obvious that the capital of the province would have to be moved, since all frontier forts were to be returned to the Americans. This meant that the parliament of Upper Canada would have to meet under the very guns of Fort Niagara if it remained at Niagara.

Simcoe still had dreams of establishing the capital at London on the river Thames, just as in England. But Simcoe was curtly overruled and told to start work at once on Legislative Buildings in York. This was just one more case of his advice being refused.

Of greater long-range importance was the land policy that Simcoe encouraged the Legislature to pass. He felt sure that there were still thousands in the United States who were loyal to the British crown. With generous offers of free land, Simcoe attracted a great number to Upper Canada. Simcoe's wisdom was to be vindicated during the War of 1812, when almost all of these recent arrivals remained loyal to Britain.

While the Governor visited for the last time as much of the province as possible, Elizabeth was still interested in the life and activities around her. She tasted her first pumpkin pie and found it even better with some lemon juice on it.

She also found a sure cure for indigestion. Pigeons' gizzards, dried and grated to a fine powder, were the infallible cure. Frequent visits were made to Castle Frank, and many meals consisted of roasting venison and the small red trout from the Don over an open fire.

Francis had turned five years old and in many

"Francis is five years old today."

ways was becoming an active boy. He went to school every day when the family were in Niagara and took his lunch of bread and cheese.

He was still fascinated by Indians. One of the last mentioned by Mrs. Simcoe in her diary is Jacob, the Mohawk. With scarlet leggings, and a black cloak, he cut a dashing figure. But, more than that, he danced a Scotch reel with more ease and grace than any person Elizabeth had ever seen.

Only once did Mrs. Simcoe complain about the Indians and that was because of a misunderstanding. While out riding with the Governor, she was terrified by a small group of Indians who raced up to them and discharged their guns in the horses' faces. Elizabeth's horse reared, she shrieked, but it was only the Indians' way of showing respect to their Governor.

In June they left Niagara for the last time and went by canoe around the lake to York. Colonel Simcoe had intended to have a series of inns built on all main roads. The only one completed was the one at the head of the lake, at Burlington. It was a very pleasant building with a magnificent view over the lake. The weather turned quite stormy; what Elizabeth called a "prodigious sea" came up and so they were forced to spend some days at the inn. No one regretted the delay because the area was so pleasant, with so many interesting walks.

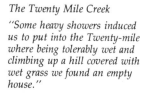

The Twenty Mile Creek

"Some heavy showers induced us to put into the Twenty-mile where being tolerably wet and climbing up a hill covered with wet grass we found an empty house."

*The King's Head Inn,
Burlington Bay*

*"This house was built by the
Governor to facilitate the
communication between Niagara
and the Thames."*

Chapter 16 **Last Days at York**

Elizabeth found it even harder to leave the small town of York than to leave Niagara. There were a number of reasons for this: the weather at York was generally less humid and both Francis and the Governor were in much better health; the scenery, while not so dramatic as that by the Niagara River, was rich in pleasant places, from the Humber to the Don; York was now to be the capital of Upper Canada, and already a number of wealthy merchants, professional

"Took leave of Castle Frank."

men, and administrators were moving there; but
perhaps the principal reason was the deep attachment
that they all had for Castle Frank.

Now that they knew they must soon leave, they
spent as much time as possible at the cottage. It was
here that they celebrated the building of the first
bridge across the Don.

It was no great engineering feat. Indeed, it was
nothing more than a butternut tree that had fallen
over the river. The branches were still on it for
support. Elizabeth was determined to be the first to
cross it, but halfway over she glanced down at the
river running under the tree, and quite lost courage.
However, as was to be expected of Elizabeth, she
determined not to let an incident such as this bother
her; summoning up her will power she successfully
crossed the river.

*"Playter's bridge over the Don
is a butternut tree, the branches
still growing in full leaf. I was
determined to cross it but was
frightened before I got half way
over."*

News came that Governor Simcoe's request for a
leave of absence was granted, and he was informed
that the frigate *Pearl* would be at Quebec City at the
beginning of August to take the Governor and his
family back to England.

July 20 was the last day that they were to spend at
York, and when the day arrived Elizabeth could not
restrain her grief. Her friends had invited her to a
farewell dinner, but for once Elizabeth's determination
deserted her. So intense was her sorrow that she was
unable to attend the dinner: "I could not eat; cried all
day."

Early on the morning of July 21, the family sailed
on the *Onondaga*. A favourable wind took them to
Kingston in a very short time, and there they
transferred to bateaux to carry them down the St.
Lawrence to Quebec City.

Elizabeth's spirits responded to the new activities
and she was soon too busy admiring the scenery and
sketching it to worry about what was now past.

The cooler air on board ship and the complete
absence of mosquitoes made life a great deal more
pleasant.

The St. Lawrence River downstream from
Kingston is little more than a series of rapids. So
swiftly did they go through the rapids at the Long
Sault that the boats appeared to fly. Elizabeth thought

they looked like racehorses trying to outrun each other. Elizabeth was terrified—but not too frightened to sketch the boats. Sometimes a whirlpool would spin the boats around, at another time the head of a boat would disappear under the water. But the sailors were skilled and the boats suffered nothing but a little water dashing over them.

The party stopped for meals at some lovely places, and the family enjoyed eating in a picnic-like atmosphere. But they were by no means through with the rapids yet.

Elizabeth found the Rapids of the Cedars "much more frightful" than those at the Long Sault. The boats rose and plunged through the white waves. Travelling along one part—"the run"—was like going down the raceway of a mill. To make matters worse, the pilot kept on stressing the dangers which only his skill could save them from. However, the men rowed with all their might and kept up a rhythmic song to time their strokes.

Once again they passed safely through. The children by now found it an exciting experience. But Elizabeth felt like crying, and this time it was the Governor, hoping to take his wife's mind off the danger, who suggested that she should sketch the scene.

The only casualty of all these rides through the rapids was Mrs. Simcoe's trunk. While being transferred from one boat to another, the trunk fell in the water. It contained all of Elizabeth's clothes, so until they arrived at Quebec she was forced to wear nothing but damp outfits. However, she proudly notes that, in spite of this, she never caught cold.

Finally they arrived at Belmont, the home of their good friends, the Caldwells, where they stayed for a few days.

For the first time in years, Colonel Simcoe was able to relax. The *Pearl* that was to take them to England was delayed, so Simcoe for once was without any special duties.

But the strain of the past few months had taken its toll of Elizabeth. Day after day her diary reads like this:

"So ill I could not go to church."

"So ill I could not go to Belmont."

"So ill I could not dine with the Caldwells."

Simcoe was still called upon in an emergency. A fire broke out in the heart of the city and he immediately organized all the men available as firefighters. Although the beautiful Recollet Church was destroyed, Simcoe's efforts prevented the fire from spreading further. The next day, as Elizabeth passed the church, she remarked that the fire, still not completely extinguished, gave "an awful, grand appearance."

On September 11, 1796 the *Pearl* weighed anchor and the Simcoe family left Canada.

Britain was at war with France and there was always the possibility that the frigate would be attacked. Indeed, for a time two French frigates pursued the *Pearl*, but the British ship evaded them and on October 14 landed at Dover.

Sophia was glad to be on dry land, but Francis, never having been seasick, was determined to be a sailor. His mother, who admired seamen, encouraged his ambition.

"We dined at Belmont, four miles from Quebec, Col. Caldwell's. A very indifferent house in appearance, but comfortable within."

Chapter 17 **Return to England**

With the return to Wolford, the Simcoe family quickly took up the activities that five years in Canada had interrupted.

During the few months he spent at home, Simcoe's interest in developing the estate was more pronounced than before his departure. Its affairs were now run on military lines, with tradesmen parading outside and servants parading inside for both morning and evening prayers.

Of course one of the great pleasures of the return was to find that the four daughters who had been left behind had developed into most lovable young people. The girls, in turn, had to become reacquainted with Sophia and Francis.

Elizabeth had brought back wonderful presents for her daughters, a carriole, a birchbark canoe, furs, and a host of other interesting presents.

Francis, now a young man of five, brought back amazing tales of his friends, the Indians.

News kept coming from Canada. John Scadding, the Simcoe's former steward, had taken up permanent residence there. He wrote of the rapid growth of York, and of the coaches that now ran between Kingston, York, and Niagara.

Bad news came about Castle Frank. Vandals tore down the fireplace and windows, and five years after their departure, the Simcoes learned that it had been burned down.

After years of frustration, General Simcoe (he had been promoted during his time in Canada) finally was offered a position where his talents had full scope. During 1797, he had shown his ability as Commander-in-Chief in San Domingo. Then he was given command of all the southern counties of England, to organize resistance to Napoleon, should he attempt an invasion. But these were all preludes to the position finally offered him, in 1806, that of Commander-in-Chief and Governor-General of India.

But this great honour was not to be his. Shortly after the appointment, as he was preparing to leave for his post, he fell sick and died after a brief illness.

Elizabeth survived her husband by forty-four years. During that time she rarely left Wolford. Tragedy struck again in 1812 with the death of Francis in Spain, where he was an officer serving under the Duke of Wellington. He was twenty-one years old.

In her old age Elizabeth became interested in works of charity. With her daughters around her, this work became one of her main sources of interest.

One of the last of the Simcoes' projects was a small chapel built in the grounds of Wolford Lodge. That chapel today has the distinction of being the only property owned by the province of Ontario outside its own boundaries.

Chapter 18 **Our Debt to the Simcoes**

Both John Graves Simcoe and his wife, Elizabeth Posthuma Simcoe, contributed much to the Canada of today. Indeed, it might well be said that Governor Simcoe was the chief architect of the country we now know.

There were many areas where Simcoe's wisdom was apparent. He saw that Upper Canada must develop along lines different from those in Lower Canada and managed to establish the customs and laws that made such development possible.

He knew that the country could not long exist without people, and his immigration policy was so successful that he was able to attract thousands of suitable settlers from the United States.

His dream of a capital city on the banks of the Thames at London never came true, but he did show that such a capital must be centrally located and some distance from the border. The site that he chose at York has developed into the great metropolis of Toronto.

Simcoe's stay in Canada was clouded by the constant threat of war with the United States. We have seen that General Wayne moved on the British fort at Detroit, and if Simcoe's preparations had not been what they were, Wayne might have moved on Upper Canada and precipitated an all-out war.

Elizabeth, too, made a contribution. Her diary, so faithfully kept during her five-year stay in Canada, has left for us a picture of the frontier that we find in no other place. We have a full record of flowers, plants, and animals. We are told of the dishes native to the land. We meet and admire the Indian, his dignity and nobility in the presence of the newcomers.

Elizabeth Gwillim, the heiress to a great fortune, showed how easily a gentlewoman of her character could cheerfully adapt to life in the New World. Elizabeth's personality was what one would expect of the wife of the Lieutenant-Governor. Her charm and her interest in everything and everyone made friends for herself and her husband wherever they went. All Simcoe's preoccupations and wishes, including his love of pageantry and tradition, were eagerly accepted by his wife.

Elizabeth died in 1850 at the age of eighty-four. Certainly, in those long years her memory must have often turned to the days when she was with her husband, the Lieutenant-Governor, in Britain's newest colony over the seas.

What debts do we today in Canada owe to Governor and Mrs. Simcoe? Based on what you have read in this book, write a character sketch of Mrs. Simcoe.

Mrs. Simcoe in Welsh costume

Further Reading

Guillet, Edwin C. *Pioneer Days in Upper Canada.* Toronto: University of Toronto Press, 1963.

_____ . *Pioneer Settlements in Upper Canada.* Toronto: University of Toronto Press, 1963. (Paperback)

Monture, Ethel Brant. "Joseph Brant, Mohawk Chief," *Famous Indians.* Toronto: Clarke, Irwin, 1960.

Riddel, W.R. *The Life of John Graves Simcoe, First Lieutenant Governor of the Province of Upper Canada. 1792-96.* Toronto: McClelland, 1926.

Scadding, Henry. *Toronto of Old,* abbreviated and edited by F. H. Armstrong. Toronto: Oxford University Press, 1966.

Simcoe, Elizabeth G. *The Diary of Mrs. John Graves Simcoe, Wife of the First Lieutenant-Governor of the Province of Upper Canada, 1792-6.* Edited by J. Ross Robertson. Toronto: William Briggs, 1911. Facsimile edition published by Coles Publishing Company, Toronto, 1973. (Also available as paperback.)

Smith. J. K. *Alexander Mackenzie, Explorer: The Hero Who Failed.* Toronto: McGraw-Hill Ryerson, 1973.

Credits

The author wishes to express his sincere appreciation of the generous assistance and scholarship always readily offered by Mr. A. Murdoch and Miss Margaret VanEvery of the Archives of Ontario.

The publishers acknowledge their gratitude and indebtedness to the following who have given permission to use copyrighted illustrations in this book:

The Metropolitan Toronto Central Library, pages 5, 6 and 8.
The J. Ross Robertson Collection, Metropolitan Toronto Central Library, page 3.
The Public Archives of Canada, page 6.

All Mrs. Simcoe's drawings are reproduced by courtesy of the Archives of Ontario.

Editing: Laura Damania
Design: Jack Steiner
Cover Illustration: John Lasruk

Every effort has been made to credit all sources correctly. The authors and publishers will welcome any information that will allow them to correct any errors and omissions.

John M. Bassett is Consultant—Communications at the Lincoln County Board of Education